NEEDVILLE

Poems by
Sara M. Robinson

Cedar Creek Publishing
A Virginia Publisher of Virginia Books
www.cedarcreekauthors.com

Printed in the United States of America

Library of Congress Control Number 2019913255

ISBN 978-1-942882-03-9

Needville, an anthology of enduring lives in the Appalachian coalfields, is a lyrical portrayal of wit and witness, interwoven with various poetic forms and drama. Combining ekphrastic art with an attentive eye and ear, Robinson recaptures the powerful stories and voices of real people—what is saved and lost—in small American mountain towns. A mesmerizing evocation of the unseeing world, from the mineral to the biological and to the spiritual, reaffirms the strength of humanity in its kinship to the unquiet earth and the role of poetry in revealing the inner workings of man and nature. The reader will find in *Needville* an unforgettable collection of Robinson's album poems that recalls Edgar Lee Masters' *Spoon River Anthology*.

– GILLIAN HUANG-TILLER
University of Virginia-Wise

Like the river to which she likens truth in "Coal Town Haiku," Sara Robinson's new collection "coils around trees & stumps / clear as coal is black." These poems intone a truth that is insistent and visceral: a tapestry of coal country voices and an inventory of daily living in coal communities, as well as an exploration of the boulder of political forces pinning these Appalachians firmly in poverty. *Needville* weaves, geography, industry, and imagination into a contemporary ballad for a people who have nearly burned themselves out lighting the nation.

– JULIE HENSLEY
Professor of Creative Writing
Bluegrass Writers Studio
Department of English and Theatre
Eastern Kentucky University

Needville is a remarkable work, characterized by compassion, anger, intensity, and poetic fluency. It has been a memorable experience to read these poems.

– JAMES FERGUSON
Professor Emeritus of English
Hanover College

These poems sing a hardness and sadness, but reveal and renew with a lightness of spirit even as they weigh on us.

– STEPHEN K. WHITE
James Hart Professor Emeritus, Dept. of Politics
Fellow, Institute for Advance Studies in Culture
University of Virginia

Table of Contents

Introduction

I fell in love with Wise, Virginia and its associated University. How did I do that? I believe my poetic imagination allowed me to develop this persona and tell the story. Under the guise and luster of my corporate life in the minerals industry I could only imagine a rough life there, protected by a beauty most do not see. This area of the state is not just a land full of hillbillies and addicts. What an insult. It is an area of living, breathing people surrounded by stately mountains, ambitious fauna, and elegant flora.

The noble professors who located there from far away states, and the local graduates, who, after pursuing advanced degrees, came back to teach their own, inspire me. They amaze and humble me with their passion. I hear the young students talk of hopes and dreams, which do not include coal, and I feel such tenderness for them. I heard a young woman read my poem, "Last Night You Asked Why I Write Poetry," in her lilting drawn-out mountain accent. I was charmed. If hope is contagious, I want to be the vector.

To write poetry about Southwest Virginia and surrounds is a daunting undertaking. I have to step out of my own comfort level here in central Virginia and place my mind and spirit in the geography and population of an area in which I have only visited. Does that make me an interloper or disingenuous? I can't say. But I do have a mining industry background, having spent about 30 years in the non-energy mineral industries. I saw first hand the after-effects of mining as well as the intrusion of equipment into ancient mountains and flatlands to seek minerals. I've been underground and in open pits. I saw residents, with homes along the truck routes, repair their cracked chimneys, barely attached to clapboard houses; and shake their fists at our drivers. When we go after our minerals we have one sight in mind, where the veins are; and how to get them out profitably, and safely. In that order. I know some things, and I wish I didn't.

When you sell minerals by the ton, and the price is less than $100 per ton, every cost has to be considered. You don't see these mines in high value landscapes. Why is that? Is it some coincidence that mines and their associated reserves are typically found in places where most people don't live or want to live? Then somehow these very folks become necessary distractions when they complain about blasting noise or polluted air and water. We want them to work in the mines yet we figure out a way to dismiss them, never mind insuring them. Why is that?

I look to Walt Whitman to express what I want to say: "O I know that those men and women [are] not for nothing, any more than we are for nothing, / I know that they belong to the scheme of the world every bit as much as we now belong to it."

If this is yet another book about the devastation and plights of the coal mining area then add this to the growing list. I want to bring attention by my anger, my descriptions, my fiction, and my desire to give this region's people respect. If my language can press others into action then I'll be thankful for my words. Will my poetry be sufficient enough? I can hope.

We all need to take care of each other, even if it is in small ways, moving one rock at a time, to make way for our words and our voices.

I dedicate this book to my dear Carolyn; to the University of Virginia's College at Wise; to the singers, writers, and speakers of Appalachia.

Sara M. Robinson 2019

A Miner to Miners

You had no way to know how you made me smile.
I had promised our folks we'd get by & see them some day
tell them we were fine, but somehow I never did.
With bosses who yelled "keep mining," & job journals
to keep, I supposed I could work by myself, but it suited me
best with you alongside me, so that I warn't alone.

You see my hand, the one with the broken joints?
I can move it when I don't mind the pain.
Did you ever feel pain so hard? I hope you never. I
don't want you to know the pain of the shovel or the pick,
but if you have to use one, choose the pick. It will
work hard along with you, more than the lazy shovel.

See the water at the end of the tunnel? Maybe you can't
at first; it's the eyes that have to adjust. The black is so
black there is no color darker. Feel the shine
of the tiny river, it moves slow like a lake on a calm
day. Down here doesn't know anything about breezes
or storms to stir it up. Filled by old trickles leaking
from walls, it waits to fill, then waits for more. Like me.

Some of the miners before you went mad after a few
weeks of working underground. Some took their picks
& slammed into other fellows. One got his head clean
swiped from his body. Funny about that blood, it
looked shiny like the little lake, but then it had this iron
smell & that was even worse, so I heard. Me? I
was at the other end & missed some of those
who went over the side. I see how that might could happen.

But I had to tell myself this is just a business, me picking
at rocks, somebody hauls them off, somebody cleans them
up, somebody sells them, & in the end they get burned up.

Continued

Sort of like me thinking that if there is a Hell it gets its burn
from all the coal that's buried here. So, you & I work from
daybreak to day's end. Might as well be happy enough in our
own thoughts. Anyway there ain't no profit on our side.

I could tell you enough stories about the mines to give you
thoughts about staying or going, but then every life & every
work has its share. Here we are & we do the best we can.
Now pay no attention to shouts you hear from the other shafts.

You keep your eye on that little yellow bird
in the cage hanging off that load car. If you see it fall
then you get the hell out of here. That bird can smell white

damp & we can't. Until then keep your pick swinging &
coal chunks tumbling. Think of wild flowers outside
& the first day of huntin' season, which we do get off. Your
wife will be happy to cook that rabbit if you skin it first.
Look. Mind that shovel over in the corner. Don't step
on the spade, knock yourself crazy. See, it's just another
day's work. Maybe we won't get ahead, but we're here.

Think about the worst you can do than mine. Me too.
I think about it all the time, & still can't imagine it.

I

"It always amazes me
How landscape recalibrates the stations of the dead,
How what we see jacks up
                              the odd quotient of what we don't see."

– Charles Wright from *The Appalachian Book of the Dead*

"For poetry makes nothing happen: it survives
In the valley of its saying where executives
Would never want to tamper; it flows south
From ranches of isolation and the busy griefs,
Raw towns that we believe and die in; it survives,
A way of happening, a mouth."   ---W.H. Auden

Mining the Mountains
Explosives and machines are destroying Appalachian
peaks to obtain coal. In a West Virginia town, residents
and the industry fight over a mountain's fate.
Source: John McQuaid, *Smithsonian Magazine*, January 2009

Where to start:

Holding a neighbor's baby boy
who felt like a puppy & looked
like one, too. Big hands.
Then on *The Americans* I saw
Philip chop a hand off, then
another, then the head.
Sort of like going from
sublime to non sequitur.

There is this photo in my head:
a man coughs up a black lung
smiles & spits at the glistening
glob on his porch. He turns
to the photographer   says
*I was only using one
of 'em anyway.* (but what
if that glob was his good lung?)

Does a meth-addicted coal town
girl look up at the night sky
& wonder why she is here?

Ghosts of miners seem to me
to have a purpose that has nothing
to do with coal.

How to stay warm in cold caves,
how to hold your breath, or
deep dive to freedom.

If the loveliest music is music
that cannot be played, then maybe
the loveliest poem is one
still trapped in the *aether*
has not descended into words.

Overburden

I found an ordinary rock
leftover from some pile
of other rocks but somehow
missed.   Left behind.
The rock did not speak
nor did it move. It was
inactive. Not passive.

When I start to write
my hand is like the rock.
But then I lift

my pen. That's when
the rock moves.

Life and Death

My feet stay cold
in black water

like some blood's trickling
in hard rock veins

I'll die too young
to see my age

There Are No Etchings Or Petroglyphs

on mine shaft walls.

Once a mountain is gutted / it is gutted
like a deer   but with no shaman

to read the entrails & foretell
a prosperous future.

Once beneath the mountains
hidden micro-verses

prospered   protected progressed
nurtured roots of flora to feed

masses for   eons   millennia.
Look at cracked fingernails

of hard-scrabble miners & tell
them if you can read a fortune.

Tell them when prosperity
will return   don't give them scrip
pretend it is real / money

burnt sienna mammoth centered

Blackwater

When coal mining came to town
the locals went to the meeting hall
expecting to hear some good
news for a change. Money.

The collection plate in reverse.
Good money for good land.
But when the city-gal spoke
the locals were not pleased.

Talk from her just didn't ring right,
like a cracked bell from the old Brethren
Church down by the creek where we
swam all our youth among tadpoles.

Maris Lam stood up & spoke
for all of us when she said:
You don know our ways…
You don know our food…
You don know our land…

Our kin built these homes…
Our parents courted in these hollers…
Our dead is buried on the tops so's they…
Can look out for us…

Now you say you gon cut our trees…
& flatten our peaks…
& you'll be good bout it?
You think we don know nothing?

I know why you call them mining
leftovers, 'spoils'.

Ther'll be no spittn' in our sprang waters…

We see their future running
down a hillside leaving trails
black as tar & as dead
as the graves beneath them.

Compression

Where in inner earth are the last remaining etchings?
Are they so compressed we won't find them
like how years of settlement & construction
keep pushing down old structures?

I want to pick up some discarded piece of coal, compress
it in my fist as hard as I can in hopes that when I open
my palm there will emerge this diamond, this perfection.

But when I open my palm, all I will see
is my sweat glistening on the surface
of this same lump which in its own struggles

etches dust on my palm. It shows: *Don't forget
me.* My petroglyph. I see dust engravings
on every burdened & burned miner's face
at the end of a ten-hour shift. Into my mind

are carved pictures of lungs, & streams wobbling
around derelict little towns. I want to rub & rub
until I see my white skin   back to something pure.

I need to feel the dust. Or look into
the eyes. It's the eyes. It's always the eyes.

The Idea of Ore in Dante, Virginia

Something sang below stopes ahead of mantle
with pumps not yet in place   but positioned
on paper, like pre-nuptial agreements, in binders.
Engineers cast their marks & thoughts
(lined in #2H pencil) out loud, too loud to hear
a song barricaded in rock.

What antecedent remains in vanishing
mountaintops is not like rising & setting
of the sun. It comes to us everyday with
light to make history. Take off that top.
All that remains in the light is raw. Tailings
are history revealed as mine offal.

A mountaintop is not a charade,
no pretense for barren pits to follow.
Surface moss facades cover hidden chords
level by level not yet exposed, too carnal
for humans. Some pre-history comes into
gasping clanks, noisy clinkers, & rock
cleavages   not attractive   not sexy.

For eons silent ferns, tremendous reptiles
mingled voices heard by prey, foragers,
& predators whose tramplings leave
paths worn into surface ruts
until chaos wrought from fiery sky.
Tortured songs of the destruction,
painful births, agonies, fueled
by extremes of heat & pressure melted
into rock & forged carbons. Then all rested.

Seeping waters trapped in mineral-filled
crevices cooled pockets which flowed

Continued

to veins. Over & over this cycle continued.
Compression into rock. Rock to ore…

Pushings rewarded sleights of hand under
continental thighs like sly lovers. Such theatrics
not recorded in script but existed only
as graphite or coal, precursors to write
down what we now know: mountains
give birth but it is rough, not pretty—

furious, helpless, & everlasting.

Pocohontas Sings a Sad Song

So tell me, Pocahontas,
do you care for us who stole
you from your perch & carried you
into dark shafts? Your magic way
is to sense the secret gas as
humans hear your silence & flee.

Your vacant perch seen too late
after your last mournful tweet.

Oh, little yellow warbler, your last
gasp   alone.

You Will Always Want:

some of the rock so buried you have
to blast it up out of the selfish ground
next to where neighbors hands over ears
lean down to pick up another chimney brick
every time a trucker rumbles & changes gears.

> *I have ridden with the drivers under orders*
> *from our chief to mitigate the damage*
> *& soothe hardening feelings. But as they*
> *stood out in the heat shaking their fists*
> *& their heads I felt what we were doing*
> *might actually be wrong.*

What lies underneath the ground: Is it meant
to stay buried or does it creep out—the poison
ivy, that it is, to leave its blistering mark?

Un-Hilton Hotel at the End of the World

There is a strong possibility that no hotels
will be built over abandoned coal mines.
For one thing there is no way to under-
dramatize an entrance that goes black.

Gilded doors to a dark pit are not exactly
inviting to expensive cars rolling up
to discharge eager guests. Who would
these guests be anyway? Who wants

to see abandoned shafts lined with old
safety helmets & a few dead canaries?
Is that coal dust floating in my martini?

The hotel annex offers another
option more satisfying: How about

a faux-claimed mountain top?
It is already flat   no cost
for tree removal   It has
already been scoured clean. No worries

about trees to block the view which
is likely to be another mountaintop
previously mined & still under
recovery. See the pretty seedlings

struggle to survive? See the
naked creeks with muted pulses drift
over forlorn boulders where empty
pools await a hint of life, perhaps

some moss. This non-hotel
will remain lonely & desperate as
we view the demise of land we love.

Continued

Is there comfort in lower energy costs
in places far removed from us where
they don't wonder about our trees? No one
takes a picture of this vacation spot which
is not a vacation spot from a hotel which

is not a hotel which is at the end of this world
which is not the world we knew.

Albino

It's tough to miss an albino white tail
against the coal mountain backdrop

she must run for her life & if there
is any kind of Ozark luck she will
mate with a dark hairy fellow & end
the curse that is her color

This color would save her on a winter
meadow's snow where she could graze

But meadows are covered now
in pipelines & rigs   scaffolds
spools of silver wire   rusted
yellow earth movers   alongside
black rubber tires   stacked
in piles leaning   overly right

Not enough time for deer to evolve
from a mutant gene to grey-black
or yellow to blend in with landscapes

which will change   too   so any
mutation will be ineffective

Probably best that she die before
she breeds we don't want

misfits to appear & interrupt
the natural course of things

like bringing up fossil fuel
to a surface whose occupants
still haven't decided whether
or not coal or gas is needed
or wanted

What do deer know anyway

Crushers & Fossils

After a mountain is topped/cut-off/robbed
of its coal, what lies beneath is exposed.

It's like sunburn & blisters. Underneath
skin abrasions/invasions/insults there is
the beauty of a person.

There is no cure for either, but people can
cover skin, hiding essentials, but mountains
with no skin & no essentials are left

exposed. What is left to love? When
miners come out of the shaft covered in
black we still see their eyes. Dust will
wash off. Skin remains. Pink returns.

Deep inside the mountain vitals are
excavated as if they were organs removed

from some cadavers, but to kill mountains,
crushers come in to finish off remains
like a pack of wild dogs picking over

leftovers that humans have
tossed out carelessly heartlessly
ignorantly   pathetically.

Who cares when fossils are used up?
Some say there will always be something
else to dig for & it will be as black.

We read the bones. We study fossils.
We will learn. We have the light.
Its distant glow might save us.

All the Dogs in Coal Town Are Black

The mountain heaves & bleeds through
veins, skin, & muscle exposed to all. Its
body carved up & divided into rock & dust.

Dogs wander empty streets & seek
places to roll off the dirt. This black dirt
sometimes burns. All is barren, sterile.

Miners come out of the shaft
covered in black dust.
Heads hung low & empty
eyes search for home, like dogs.

Both forage for leftovers where
there are none. What little they find
is so black so endless, like loss
of hope. Removal does rash things

to rocks, humans, & dogs. With nothing
left to forage, where do dogs go in coal
town but to some porch where they can
crawl or slide under & wait…

See the moon…
everything burns…   through dust…

Cave

The morning the first hole was blasted
dust was blown into the air
& a thousand bats were hurled
awake, thrown out of the dark.

A million squeals we heard. In their
jammed radar they rushed into
trees   dump trucks   coal haulers
before to the ground, stunned.

Like soldiers trying to make it back
to safety, they struggled & dragged
broken arms & torn skin, never to fly.

A scooper came along, picked them up
in three moves & dumped all
into a trash bin. No one said a word.

Like no one speaks when they see lesser evil
trample over perceived greater good.

The Root of Faults

Mountain of no roots
slips ledge by ledge
bench by bench
into the bitter water

where a shore once
held birch & willow

where ducks drifted
among long grasses

as trout sneaked in
& out of cover

until a leap snared
a dragonfly

mountains move
with nary a tendril
to hold them back

faults of tension
create masses doomed
to extinction

how to stop a tremble
before it starts:

begin with the roots

II

"If I ponder too long the wide mouth of an abandoned mine
I will choke on unheard gasps & breaths floated out on dust.
I want to take each man & woman cling to their voices,
tell them to leave, never come back. These mountains
will kill you in revenge for their own needless deaths."

– J. Burton Hollifield from *Water Run Down the Mountain*

"In 2009, Massey Energy, at the time the largest coal producer
in Appalachia, sponsored a West Virginia Labor Day rally
attended by 100,000 people; Don Blankenship, then the
company's CEO, assured the crowd that 'global warming is
pure make-believe.'"
– *Coal: A Human History*. Basic Books. 2003 & 2016.
Barbara Freese. p. 256.
(Note: Blankenship was later indicted by federal grand jury for
conspiring to routinely violate mine safety standards at a mine where
twenty-one miners were killed in 2010. Ibid.)

Haiku Graffiti on Underground Coal Cars

Where milkweed grows tall
behind an abandoned mine
look for my angel

Missing full lunch box
return soonest to Freddy
you can keep the cake

Crushed thermos found here
beside dented hard hat &
worn broken-toe boot

Someone smelled some gas
canary left on Tuesday
don't stop for the flash

Wise birds always trump
when it comes to detection
of odorless gas

Graphite as Contortions

Graphite forms into contorted shapes
through no will of its own—
I can write with it, as it only
leaves its mark when pressed

I push a pencil from side to side
if I am lucky & the carbon bends
the contrails of my action legible
words of verse will shape-shift

Graphite could be useful to me
even though it is black slick
& sometimes tubes are squeezed
to grease the workings of clocks
& locks of gates to keep things
                    in or out

Graphite can cleave into separate
shapes   but even with its softness
graphite writes hard words describes
hard things hard coal it has a tough life—
things do move   when pressed enough

Carbon Paper

All the ink has to do is stay on the tip of a finger
the art will create itself if the beholder has any eye

at all for what he is about to do: mix pounded roots
into red clay with old dead ashes result is blue-black

with a few beetle carapaces scrunched & scarped
sienna will capture the herds that hunters missed

but preserved as art   in caves   now hidden
among veins of something the future will take

as more important than any record of prior life

the future will see carbon in one way &
poets will give up their anger in another

Every time   i turn   on a light

start a load   of wash

watch Netflix   i

feel   some shame

in a place   away   from me

a wagon of coal   is emptied

into a coal carrier   railed

to a power plant   which

makes electricity   for me   for you

the instant   my coffee maker

clicks on   at 7:15   my first

thought is   not of the coal miner

who   carries his coffee

in a battered thermos

while i drink mine   out of

a hand-cast   ceramic collectible

my first thought is   i see the sun

i should think   about what he

sees   but i don't like to drink

in the dark   who does   no one should

Sub-terranean Poetry

For underground poetry
to become relevant—
it must develop a purpose
like a jaw-clenching machine
which breaks coal from rock

its lines must liberate diamonds
from dust & create verse from gems

To sanctify scalped mountaintops
broken pencils & dried-up pens
must write prayers
to leave as petroglyphs
so some gods will
blow forgiveness
down shafts &
scour everything

How Are Poets Like Geologists?

Both are famous for:

picking up two or three stones

sketching or writing
an entire epic odyssey

both can render an era
into a vast landscape

where no one thought

life had existed or no one
had ever seen before

such are lines & their faults
either written or hidden

pen or pick hits the terrain

Coal Town Haiku

I
Streets always run dark
like old streams viewed at midnight
Blackened, burned, mined out

II
What the needle holds
clear liquefied wet dreams
No reason to live

III
She sees the window
through this she watches the night
moon shines on scarred vein

IV
Another meth head
sees light but not much else here
Flash to the lighter

V

Truth is a river
that coils around trees & stumps
clear as coal is black

Thermodynamic Body Hidden in a Miner

He feels his body electric
& it comes from some-
where so deep: a place
bound in rocks layers

that when hacked to
life   its energy is
boundless   but finite

to care for this body
is not within the scope
of his humanity

he buys & eats to live
he knows his time
will be brief   intense

he wants to worship
speed & life   but
there are so many

out there who tell
him he has plenty
of time   he doesn't

combustion & compression
pressure & release
those elusive atoms—
keepers of toil
fortune tellers
of early death

In a Mine Shaft

Talk of coal while hauling rocks—
carts full   on rails where others
horseshoe-bent can't gaze upward
only listen for instructions
directions   single syllables
caught up in the why & how
of this place

A shout from below, *I see your face,*
Carl, who neither smiles nor frowns
masked anyway by coal dust as he
floats   present & weighty as
stone   in his lungs   & if his
lungs could speak to the dust:

> *I know why you are here*
> *& that is not for love of me*

The Next-to-Last Canary Speaks

It's a moment.
Our lives are a moment.
It's between those moments
we live,
a space of time
between the blinks
where we crowd in
our tears   laughs   great books
not-so-great poems
& all else that fits.

It's a moment
between solar cyclones,
between trips to the store,
where among the aisles
we pause   hoping to
choose one or two things.

Between the finish line
& the thirteen steps,
before when we
hear something,
a sharp sound.

this moment   this immense
space   between other moments
where we take a
measure with no markings

creates another space
with no defined depth
or width, but great heights
over which we cannot
see the moments
we forgot to count.

Until this one:
this immeasurable moment,
where time yawns
like a big cat
after he swallows
the next-to-last
canary whose moment
stopped suddenly.

And on the Eighth Day It Rained

I
We want you here
until we don't

II
Coal ash rests on anyone's skin
makes everyone brown or black

III
When it is dark inside
coal gas smells the same

IV
A mountain in winter
covered with snow
doesn't looked scalped

V
In cities far away
families read by firelight

VI
In cities close by
fires are underground

VII
Poets cry words
as they write

VIII
There is a sweet poem
about all this
trapped in a deserted hollow

Lateral Pressures: Contractions

Forces of infinite power: Flexures and fractures
Displacements: Shovings

I.

And you thought I was writing about coal
Maybe you thought this was the start of
a political lyric, but in both cases you
would be wrong. I am writing about

what goes on inside my brain when
I compose lines while watching
straight line winds, CNN, & rain pound
against my office window. I hear
drops bazooka-blast glass as if nature
was pissed that these molecules
allowed themselves to be caught,

then formed into something through
which man can view the world. What
else would these minerals be good
for? How best to see what is going
on, rather than face the unknown
blind. Would coal look black through
a glass in an alternative universe?

Consider this looking glass:

We see one way, for now, because
it would take magic for our molecules to line
up so precisely, for us to walk through
the glass & if we did   what would we see
if we could look back.

Continued

44

II.

Shovings

the   political

nature

is

to see

one way

for us to

walk

* *Shovings* is an erasure poem version of
"Lateral Pressures: Contractions"

Quantum Poetry

There was no poetry before the existence
of time & space

BUT what if poetry were sub-atomic?
   Magical   mysterious   provocative
         capable of passing through mountains

to suddenly appear on the other side

Some grand unifying line driven at
      metrical foot speed   form shifting

genius genre   holding in its elements
no cure for philosophy   but one for

black lung disease   (which dwells
      in the depths of mines)

This is the fourth dimension:

      where one wants to wish for
            curative air that smells of cinnamon

            & is frozen in time

III

He talks of coal, hauling the rocks
cart-full to the rails where others
horse-shoe bent can't gaze upward

only listen for instructions, delusions,
illusions, single syllables, caught
in the why and how of their place.

I see your face, Donny, you neither smile
nor frown, masked by coal dust as it
floats ever present in the dank air

weighty as stone in your lungs.

– S. Robinson from *Coal River Elegy*

"Over time, past generations have had deep conflicting feelings about coal. It's been seen as a mark of poverty and as the epitome of fashion, as an annoying nuisance and as the foundation of human progress, as a sinister substance linked to a demonic underworld and as a destiny-shaping gift from God." *Coal, A Human History*. Basic Books. 2003 & 2016. Barbara Freese. p. 247.

"U.S. coal consumption in 2018 was at its lowest levels in 39 years, according to [a] recent EIA report. More coal-fired plants closed in Trump's first two years in office than in the entirety of Obama's first term." *The Washington Post*. January 29, 2019. Catherine Rampell.

Wants & Needs

Ask a coal mining family what they want
and they will give you a list (not ranked):
faster cars
warmer houses
rare art
drugs
teeth
normal feet that work
all-you-can-eat buffets
Walmart gift card
a way out
dog, any color but black
running water, clear
husband home

Ask again what they need (not ranked),
usual household staples:
meth   to get by
coal   to get heat
Coke   to stop thirst

puppies   to love
Luckys   to breathe
sweet air   to sing
the check
indoor plumbing
wood to feed the stove

wish list for a future

How Do the Poor *Feel Poor* in Needville?

they have:
outdated cell phone
used microwave
Atari game console
slow internet
analog TV
big satellite dish
half-empty Early Times bottle

& they:
still smoke
play Powerball
buy Bud-Lite & cheap whisky
eat fast food
scramble toward all-you-can-eat buffets
don't work out
have cancer of the mouth
wait in long lines for the free clinic

hope

Homer's Ghost

The ghost of Homer Isaac "Pup" Chase
watched a wife cook green beans.
Fatback sizzled & jumped in the old
black skillet, played leap-frog with
collards & spit at the stove. It
was a large skillet meant to feed
a mother & five youngsters while
they waited for their Pop. He was

down a couple of miles hammering
at the last vein in the long run where
the big diggers couldn't reach. It
was barely light & so quiet you
couldn't hear anything but a distant
dripping.

This ghost present most days can't
tell the mom of dangers below but
she likely knows. He can't tell her
he no longer eats but is always
hungry. His hands are black
& nails are split to the quick.
He sleeps under the house with one
of the black dogs & a couple of
racers coiled underneath insulation.

His hat light doesn't work but it
still sends out a ray which only
he can see. She hears something

when she looks up from the stove.
A rustling kinda noise in a corner.
The kids busy coloring on the floor
don't hear it. She feels something
like   flannel   stops   catches her breath.

She knows their Pop will not come
out of the mine   fatback burns.

Mammoth

When he reached the end of the shaft
the temperature turned arctic freeze—
there was no vent but there was a
vein of solid ice & as he pointed

his light into the crevice he saw
something brown encased in the
clear stone— when he looked

closer still & even as he approached
hairs on his neck rose in awe
(not fear) for what he found.

He could not speak as he showed
his light from one end to another,
then he realized it was something
from THE past   our past   he

dared to touch the mammoth
head   encased   motionless
as if they both were frozen

for a few moments   he knew
he was more than a miner in southwest
Virginia   he was an explorer
far beyond the dreary work of picking
coal   he could brag of this
for what was left of his mining
life: He would be someone.

Who Owns the Rights Under My Bed

Under my house layers of mud & clay
cloak the minerals that owners of big
plants want. Until they tell me to move.

I am a tenant holder of the space—
they could take my bed,
my hunting dogs, my rifles, hell
they could take my pretty wife.

I don't own my house & I barely
own my life. Each summer the fixers
appear & we wait to see where their
trucks will stop. We know time is up

when the tripod comes out & is set up
in the middle of the fields. They
smash the corn & beans like
they were pesky briars or mullein.

Sent by the coal companies their job
security is set as long as there is land
to measure. We wait. We wait.

When I sleep in my bed in my house
over land I don't own, I pretend this
is all a dream until the alarm goes
off at the foreman's house.

Summoned like cattle, we gather &
wait for the elevator to take us below
where we see what they own. We pick
at their veins while they drain from ours.

We all will turn to carbon & silica someday.

Dark

It is dark & broken in a coal mine.
as dark as inside the mouth
        of a meth addict. Rotten
teeth as broken as chunks of carbon
which fall randomly into buckets
hauled to a waiting surface.

Broken teeth fail to talk or cry
or make sense of a local landscape.

There is no escape plan for this one
or for coal which is valued so much
more than the other.

Coal provides energy. Another consumes
energy. Both destroy people. Some die
early. Some die in pain. Both would
live longer with a fix.

O, but this fix is a dark place. A shaft
or a syringe. Both dwell in dark confines.
Tunnels with no light. Just ends.

Black

I

Wrap my bones in carbon paper
tamp them down
then pull off the paper   a square
    at a time
leave the black on these bones
as witness I was a miner

II

Black imprints fit on what is left
remains follow the earth
much longer than my sweat

III

Take the paper & burn to ash
spread that ash around my grave
in a circle filled with mine shafts

IV

I started & ended in the mines
carbon all around me
black   black   black
I never left

Favorite Month

Do coal miners & their families notice
fall colors or only disappointment when
the November frostiness descends?

Before they pretend to believe
in Spring they must get beyond
the hardest months, see through
soot, & days of monochromatic
greys outlined by even greyer lines.
Blends all fall to charcoal & steel.

We cannot ask them for their favorite
month. There is no month called Grey.

Economic Evangelism

In Needville, haves & have-nots vie
for small things like coins, battle hard
for big tickets like cars & double-door LGs.

Economic evangelism as new philosophy brought
to us by ministers who preach that wealth is
divine destiny so precious & pure that
only a special few can attain it.

What is more establishment than religion? What is
worshipped more, coveted more, fought over more,
than money? Let us pray.

No prayer request was ever denied that came with
a check. God wants special people to be rich.
There is no place in provenance for poverty.
Let us bow our heads; close our eyes.

The glare of gold's radiation seeps out of the earth
& reaches past our outstretched arms.

…Blinds us…

Lemon With Your Water

Do you think you can get a lemon slice
for your water in Minden, West Virginia?
Something to cover up the taste of
mercury left over from coal mining.

Nothing masks the taste of good ol'
bitterroot in the aquifer more than
an ample dash of plentiful synthetic
chemicals. What? You thought these

were harmless? All the focus on lead
in the upper Midwest & down here
in the empty bowels of America where
coal was once king, queen, surrogate,
& moneychanger, no one noticed cancer

implanting itself among the working people
& getting away with it, 'cause (frankly)
no one gave a shit, you know. After all
these folks are about as invisible as you
can get back behind ridges & deep in the
recesses of forgotten land. Only one

by-product of coal production: Atrophy:
the slow disintegration, withering vegetation.

No ball teams, no tuna casserole church
suppers, & no little skinny-legged
burlap-wrapped green-faced ninjas
in October with Dollar General bags
begging for Snickers & Hershey bars.

Yep, lemon-flavored anything would
taste about right.

Needville

Where is the loneliest place on earth?
You walk into an all-night 7-Eleven.
All you want is a 6-pack of Bud Lite, $5.99.
What they have–that's cold–is Shiner Bock,
$9.99, which means you can't get peanut
butter nabs you planned for your dinner.
So now you are stuck with this
premium beer & no money in Pound.
It's that tough.   Like once:

I saw a guy come into this Italian
place in Big Stone Gap, 1969. It's
11PM, they're going to close but this
guy–he's drunk–says he'll buy a whole
pizza. Owner says they're closing & pizza
is frozen. Guy says it don't matter
he'll take it. I just watch. Then I
leave while he's still in there begging
for that frozen pie. It's sure tough. Like:

this time in Bristol, Virginia 1975,
I'm in this fish camp–my regular
Friday night out–I know the owners
& they know me. It's a mother, her
son & daughter-in-law. I'm happy
in a booth & notice this couple up
at the bar. They're drinking beer
& eating raw oysters. The more he
drinks the louder he gets. Little while
later I notice them get up to leave.
She goes to the ladies room, he walks
to the front. As I exit I see him
argue with the mother about paying

Continued

the bill. He says his girlfriend
has the money when she comes out.

Girlfriend arrives, asks what's going
on, he says she's to pay the bill, she
says she thought he would pay;
she doesn't have any money. Then
he throws something; mother calls
for help & a fight breaks out. I tell
the girl to come outside with me so
she won't get in trouble. Now police
have arrived. The help have taken this guy
outside & he throws a punch at me.

I'm laid flat. He's arrested for assault
on the mother & police ask if I want
to press charges; but they tell me I have
2 years to do this. There's a trial.
Guy is found guilty. Judge asks me why
I didn't press charges & I say I wanted
to see what kind of sentence he got.
Judge throws book at him.
It's still tough.   Like:

For years I had nightmares about that night, & I
never went back to that fish camp. Now all this
is a poem: the loneliest place on earth is
the backside of a memory, which is always
dark—always in need. When you wake up
you feel it—inside it burns—outside it's slimy.

Life in the *'Burbs*

In the outskirts of Pocahantas, Stephens, Verda, or Evarts
there are no tract houses with two-car garages, exotic wood
decks or outdoor kitchens, unless you count burn barrels.

Exterior decorations are bars on windows & doors. The
poorest areas have the most of these as my philosophy
is those with little, steal from those who have less.

You find men with just enough to live on 'til Judgment
Day. They work all the time. They know the risk of
a shortened life in order to get enough to live on.

Who sees this:

    Endless cycles of dark, sun, dark, dark, dusk, black moods.

Coins of this realm are not shiny. New currency is delivered
up the interstate   where it is spread around more   so when
it does come back here   it's already been touched   a lot.

Fog Hangs Down in a Mountain Hollow Town

When fog hangs in a coal town does it reflect "white"
in headlights? The white of hope? Or does it
envelope everything in a dirtied mist of big drops
so dark   a bleak absorption   which reminds you
that you will never leave the mines. You sing an
old tired country cliché: *You will always stay no matter
where you go.* A thousand chest x-rays from

this moment will remind you that coal dust is
forever. Fog keeps it around. If dust doesn't kill
you it will certainly nag you to death. When
you cough your guts up & nothing is produced
but a sore throat, the mine tells you about
everlasting love   & it always hurts.

Clinch

I wander through each dark street
near where the crooked Clinch flows

In every face I see signs of sorrow:
life too slow, hunkered down like rocks

In all the towns of all the men
cries of infants are defined by pain

It's every voice; it never ends
the manacles of thirst tighten

How the coal-diggers yell curses
as church pulleys ring blackened bells

Luckless miners flail their bloodied
hands against narrow walls & timbers

But most nights all the way through
youngsters holler out their freedom curses

Cry louder when a mine shaft blows
& over the flights of wives they scramble

to get there first   to see what they will leave.

Escape

There is no free running water in coal country—
if you are poor & live in what urbanites call
a *backyard shed* you have no connection
to needed funds or town sewer

When a real estate ad shows an abandoned
building falling down at the end of a dirt
& stone road as a house for sale under
$25,000   then you get a sense of where
values are going   it is not a good time

to buy in this part of mountain-rich
southwest Virginia   most people
are poor here   the best places to visit
are an ATM, Hardees, & Dollar General

Where folks look down on those
who cross the mountain & climb
out of the hollows to shop at Walmart

For some that *train has left the station*
& coal trains pass every day   one
boxcar might contain red   white
& blue flannel shirts   but it doesn't
unload here   bigger towns are

farther out of these valleys
trains escape   but not the people
with their starving weeping water

Lucky Strike

It's another cold morning
where the temperature
in my bones is lower than
than air coming in leaky
windows held by conduit tape

Sometimes it is hard
to move & when I
turn my head toward
the shed wall I have
to brace myself for
yet another day

by the tracks where
I search for roots:
you know the ones
that promise eternal youth
& increased smarts
ginseng roots

My cracked nails glued
together forever with clay
& silt are always eager
to dig   When I
get my money

I'll buy that precious
pack of Luckys & with
that first drag I'll think
of what a real home
is like: a yard
for my little dogs   a patch
for my horseradish

& a red geranium in a real window

Peeling Onions While Thinking of Dill

The old-aged miner dreads the slow walk home.
It is Thursday night & though he is dog-tired
his wife will greet him with *wash your hands*
then come peel onions for our stew.

All day he has inhaled coal gas & bad breaths.
His wish for the evening is to sample clean air,
but it is Thursday & on this day, every week,
they have liver & onions. He must keep up his

strength, his devoted wife says. Iron in calves'
liver is much better for him than that crap
he buys off the food truck. How can he tell
her that though she packs a good lunch

everyday, he saves some of it for when the food
truck isn't there & he can't buy his beloved
dill-flavored egg salad sandwich. Memory
of that fragrant dill is so strong if he could

wear fronds around his neck deep in the shafts
he would. Then he could abide all the strange
smells along with any other uncovered hellish scent
that gets in the way; like those he remembered

from fields in Asia years ago when he & his
platoon blasted their way through tangled jungles
searching for mines, discarded ammunition, those
abandoned cook fires & their damn steaming ramps.

The Corner of Lana Star Road & Paradise

O Kelpie, O Alantedoba, O Bormana, all who rule over land & water
please take me out of the mines & valleys   give to me
a little whisky tavern
with clever spirit labels:
    lined up according to shades of amber
    intriguing shapes   of fine glass
    stacks as still as soldiers   on terry mats

Give me back the mountains of Pocahontas & her sisters
their fine branch waters   to pour   on my head

Toss away measuring cups & pour at will & liberty
to all that enter including the meth-heads & loose
teenage girls who only want to be respected & find
a modest job; so they can shop at the local store for
treasured tank tops & boyfriend shorts

O Kelpie, O Meduna, O Bride, you must rule over all—
please bring me this quaint tavern
    where I can pour to everyone's content

Where I can forget my addiction to poetry
    devote myself to the mysteries of malt
    & cry alone for those whose thirst I cannot quench

IV

American Poetry

"Whatever it is, it must have
a stomach that can digest
rubber, coal, uranium, moons, poems."
....
– Louis Simpson from *The Owner of the House:
New Collected Poems,* 1940-2001

Canary

A young girl wanders off
from her family's cabin

late fall this 4-year old
will soon feel the spikes

of season's first snow, icy
stings, frosty caresses,
chilled-to-bone howls

not sweet lullabies. She dies
buried under drifts & leaves

In spring   a canary rises:
    the brightest yellow
            clearest voice
                    purest song

She flies into a mine shaft
descends with the miners
finds a beam   stays there

One miner sees this little
bird everyday writes
some lines in his torn
journal rubbed black

by hands with deep
crevassed nails but still
hold a pencil:

    her sweet voice
        calls me home

Continued

I beg not to cough
    in front of their mom
        my kids keep the secret:
my life will end
in a rumble   someday
but not while she sings
she must always sing

Appalachian Rose

She sang below unmined brilliance
where carbon is so dense it is no
longer known by one single letter;
for how could diamonds be described
by anything but words of glitter—
countless facets & limitless carats

Yet she warns when danger is close
so legs can run before the fumes
either choke or consume as fire

Some must escape   to live to tell
of the one rough crystal still
hidden there which when found
a century later will be named

after the long-gone flower &
warning bird whose voice
so strong sang to petals so deep
crimson like the heart of the world

Underground Economy

No running water
nearest neighbors: copperheads & rattlesnakes
disability checks: some missing some run out

old black watch plaid jacket
faded muddy torn pocket
while dogs sleep under
a faded fleece American flag blanket

jeans patched with old inner tube rubber
it's the knees   all that crawling

wedding band dented, chipped, looks
like something made from a bottle cap
probably Mountain Dew

some houses are sold as garden shacks
at Lowe's. Rite-Aid cell phones
Dollar Tree plates & soda

Where everyone is slowly weathering
in the last town buried in the last county
in the worn-out sock toe of the state

This is life at the end of a big foot:

    If the poor are forced to give up hygiene—
    last resort of dignity—what do we

    leave them with? For god's sake
don't throw a roll of paper towels
or tins of talcum powder at them then

brag you are helping   if you haven't
smelled seven days of dirty clothes

you have no clue as to
what can save a person

Mathematical Theory in Mine Shafts

When air shifts in a mine shaft
that is no time to think about algebra

The equation is simple: do not concern
yourself with balance on both sides,

get the heck out & worry about
the right side which means making

it to the elevator before the whole
thing caves or (god-forbid) blows.

In coal mining, mathematics
is not about complex differentials:

add, subtract, divide, multiply

the last two learned mostly
on Sunday from lessons
given by the preacher who

will descend into the mines
like the rest of his flock on Monday.

His pastoral wages so meager
compared to the six figures
he earns in the shafts.

It's simple arithmetic.

You Pick Your Friends

When the alarm bell goes off
& methane is loose there is no
time to be a homophobe.

Your only source of clean air
is the gay guy you came down
the elevator with this morning.

You know he is a queer because
everyone in town talks about him
and "his friend." You've never

paid him much mind till he started
work at the mine a couple of months
back. He wasn't on your crew

until this week & now he is in
your shaft loading coal
when the goddam alarm sounds.

You hear him breathe in from
the emergency tank then
he hands you the mask.

In that one second of exchange
with his kind eyes you reach
for it, then you both know

that you will live. When you
reach the surface everything will
go back to normal. He'll be

that queer guy & you'll be
the not-quite-the-same guy,
but we all know you'll
never share a Rolling Rock.

What Miners Carry

Do miners carry with them burning buildings
or perhaps burning shafts? How does fire damp
smell to them: like torched flesh? Maybe
methane smells like nothing else.

As they swing sledgehammers against
hard black veins, I wonder if they think
of Mar-A-Lago. Thoughts of a better life
may creep in with each swing, but these
compete with counting minutes during work.

Wives probably wish husbands would shower
at the plant, & not dirty the bathtub: the one
white thing they have. The closest water looks
nothing like the clear blue Caribbean.

At company parties management gives
senior miners wall clocks with tiny pick
axes for hour & minute hands, numbers
as miner hats with little lights that
blink when the hour strikes.

Most of the clocks stop working when
the batteries go dead/ Like the miners, too.

White Ghost

Too bad we couldn't grab that peat before
it became coal. We could have used it
to make wonderful savory whisky.

Its smoke would have lent itself
to a flavor unique to Appalachia:
The 25-year old Ashbourne,
double-peaty single malt

made from the murky waters of coal
dust springs & tears of those who lived
forty thousand years ago. Now
distilled in hollows by lanky

widows dressed in black wool dresses—
their eyes stay peeled toward the
highway to the mines. Sure they
miss husbands & sons but with

this whisky they cling to survival.
With each sip they take from
a bent enamel cup they can taste
a good life somewhere. Not here.

Talc: The Other Coal

I learned an important life lesson:
one body can be worth $417 million.

Did that 63-year old feel like
she won the lottery? It's a terminal

win though, she likely will
not live to spend it all.

Regrettable & very sad—
we have been told that talcum

powder causes ovarian cancer,
the cost of being clean & fresh

between showers or during our
periods when we are meant

to live in a state of attraction
with sweet smelling powders.

O, our genitals so valuable
so vulnerable, this cage

we carry them in breaks
down with nothing left

to carry us. Because something
smells good & is soft doesn't mean
it is harmless.
        Like coal: Talcum powder gives
        but it takes away.

Mined-Forged Manacles

Blacksmith shackles made from
cheap coal run-of-mine quality
hold miners in dark places
if only in their imaginations.

Coal dust causes their world
to cry blackened tears down haggard
cheeks of coal soldiers who sigh as
blood hardens in their veins thickened
by deep work   dampened by sour air.

I wander through gridded streets
near where the fatted Kanawha flows
& I check each face I see…
eyes cast down, no place to go.

I hear the cries of all the coal men
& infants who cry in cradles of cobbled
pallets covered in burlap bags, with
all the voices mixed into one sad lament
as if manacles were somehow real.

Genetic Geology

If all the genes in SW Virginia
are tied to some underground vein
which runs so close to the local
DNA, then you can't tell if a person
is rooted there or stuck in muck.

Escape may be next to impossible
when pain overwhelms the desire
to change the one life you have.

Opioids trapped in your dreams
& sweats call out with eerie cries:
    Remember your mother, call for
    your father, echo your sisters
    & brothers who came before,

maybe died too soon, left you here.
The mountains lie when they pretend
to snuggle with you 'cause underneath
is rock & its hard coal. It's dark.

Everyone wants it, not you. Lie down
think of nothing. Let your mind
go blank: the bliss of "Oxy" high
will take you away. Maybe forever.

Then again, maybe not.

1st National Bank of Needville

As a courtesy for the inconvenience
of your shortened life, vouchers will

be passed out, starting at 4:30 on Friday
or at the end of your shift, day or night.

Come by the Elks Club hut & show
your coal company-issued photo ID.

These vouchers can be redeemed by
any family member, younger than

twenty-one, upon your death.
They will be accepted at your

Burger King, Captain D's, CVS,
Family Dollar, & Sparky's Emporium.
Not good for cigarettes or beer.

Some drugs are allowed so check
with your local retailer to see what

applies.   Remember   always
carry your ID & thank you for

your service. With gratitude
from our shareholders

    & your friendly bank.

Graphite Has the Last Word

There is no graphite mined in the United States.
but we use it to write a lot as pencil stock.
Like its cousin, King Coal, it is black & is

elemental carbon. It can be both synthetic
& natural   but natural comes from Sri Lanka
with additional amounts from Mexico.

Someday graphite-rendered drawings on
a concrete wall may preserve a history of what
this civilization has left. There won't be
figures of bears, deer, hunters, or gatherers

Art will be more like scenes of people scaling a
high fence or barrier only to fall backwards
into pits of tar   while in the next panel
will be stick figures   guns pointed at

them   children kneeling hoping to be
missed by   bullets   flying through
methane-free air.

Graphite so soft   malleable   with a feel
to the touch   like grease   perhaps
pleasant to the touch   but as a pencil
its modern purpose no longer serves
for caves or rocks but is destined to give

those who write on paper part of a well-made
mechanical pencil with 0.5 mm lead for finer
points & 0.9 mm for strong points. A fine pencil

we would give a young child lifted over a wall
by desperate parents who gave up everything

Continued

so the child could   have a chance   then someday
write about how brave they were. This child should have
many pencils & Mexico should not run
out of graphite. We can pay for it.

No one wants to smuggle coal anyway from Virginia.
We feel better when we can escape in daylight.

Thanks

Will a generation from now know what a miner is?
When the "future-lennials" turn on lights they
won't think for a second about the source
of that energy? They will have acted via
their smart phones with voice-activated
software & voilà the lights will come on.

Who'll start "Thank-a-Miner Day"? How
would it be celebrated? Hot dogs & burgers
on charcoal grills or plugged-in Cuisinart
grilling machines around which everyone
extolls the miracle of electricity.

Ball caps will be given out that are white
with black coal dust spelling out names
of mines: "Make Pocahontas Great Again"
or my personal favorite: "Coal Dust Rocks".

Ah, America, it is tough to thank all the
right people when it is so much easier
to reap benefits given to us from those
who died or disappeared. We don't have
to face them. Thank them for their sacrifice.

Never ever touch an electrical outlet
with hands wet from dripping apathy.

I See Earth as Emerging Poet

Of this I am certain
I need things & I
spend a huge amount
of time searching for
them   I thought
answers would be
found in multiple
rounds of spider solitaire
but I lied   even worse
I tried to fool myself
I need to write & I
cannot put it off any
longer   there is this
thread of lines
my hand is a needle
with a huge eye that
even I can manage
to get something through

It started long before I
was born   it started long
before the earth came
about   it started some
where in a universe before
elements collided in a
predictable way to form
molecular entities   attractions
bound atoms & sub-atoms
all over the place   it was like
they needed to do this it
had to happen

this is how I explain that I am over 4
billion years old   I have very
old elements wandering around
in my body   with minute parts
that are not aging but only
changing   so I set the words
in motion   see the carbon parts
of letters form words then lines
& how this is connected to

my thinking   & my writing   my scarred & acned surface
is man-made   but I live with it
I tell about it   we cry

& I will write

Last Poem Found in Needville

"The mountain held the town as in shadow"—Robert Frost

We've picked through all the residues
all the tailings & once the coal is gone
there will not be a fossil record to burn
or to heat & comfort our children

There will be no four hundred million years
of sparks ascending in coal towers but there
will be lights across the eastern mountains
& some parts of our mid-west belly buttons

Our western neighbors will burn its natural gas
for lights & heat to read the history of coal
they won't remember anything about
the Brea tar pits where on occasion a few
scientists find a saber-tooth tiger jaw

But in the east we struggle with new energy:
the sun whose rays captured by flat energetic
shiny panels give up their random firings
to lights & heat with no sunburn effects

these platters of bounty will soon take over
fields, plains, parking lots, & building tops
black panels may even shade the tiny vole

We will always need something just out of reach
we don't invent anything into a source of energy
we find sources & figure out ways to take it
for our own services   that's what we do

We will always need this energy   it is our addiction
mining for it   is the syringe   we feel its
burn   in our lungs   on our tongues   on our hands
in our own   precious   hidden veins

Acknowledgements

Maybe it "takes a village." Maybe the village is called, "Needville." Maybe each of us as individuals form a village when we come together for the same reason. My village is my poetry and those who dwell in poetry form a village with me.

I could not have done this work without the incredible help and support of these wonderful individuals who allow me to dwell in their villages: Dr. Lesley Wheeler; Dr. Jim Ferguson; Dr. Stephen White; Dr. Margie Tucker; Ms. Barbara Freese; Ms. Patsy Asuncion; Dr. Julie Hensley; Ms. Rita Quillen; Mr. James Cole; Mr. Al Mirmelstein.

A special thanks to Dr. Gillian Huang-Teller who started me on this path some years ago when she first invited me to the University of Virginia's College at Wise.

My enduring and forever gratitude to Ms. Linda Layne for seeing the light at the end of my tunnel and helping me open it.